Compiled by The Editors at Tangerine Press.
Illustrated by Mike Wright.

an imprint of
SCHOLASTIC
www.scholastic.com

Copyright © 2004 Scholastic Inc.

Scholastic and Tangerine Press and associated logos are
trademarks of Scholastic Inc.
Published by Tangerine Press, an imprint of
Scholastic Inc; 557 Broadway, New York, NY 10012

10 9 8 7 6 5 4 3 2 1

ISBN: 0-439-68983-X

Printed and bound in U.

D0250354

Warning:
Humor may be hazardous to your bad mood!

# Chicken Stuff

Why did the chicken cross the road?
Because he was a chicken.

What did Colonel Sanders say when the chicken crossed the road?
I missed one!

What do chickens eat at birthday parties?
Coop-cakes.

Why do chickens lay eggs?
They become egg-cited.

Why did the chicken cross the state line?
To get out of Kentucky.

What do you get if you cross a chicken with gum?
Chicklets.

What happened to the little chicken that misbehaved at school?
It was eggspelled.

Why did the chicken cross
the road?
She wanted to see the
man lay a brick.

Why did the gum cross
the road?
It was stuck to the
chicken's foot.

How do chickens dance?
Chick to chick.

What happened when the
hen ate cement?
She laid a sidewalk.

Why did the man cross
the road?
He wanted to eat the
chicken.

4

Why did the rooster stay outside during the hurricane?
It was fowl weather.

Which day of the week do chickens hate?
Fry-day!

What is Superchicken's real identity?
Cluck Kent.

Is chicken soup good for your health?
Not if you're a chicken.

What happened to the chicken whose feathers were pointed the wrong way?
She was tickled to death.

Why don't chickens like people?
They beat eggs.

What is a haunted chicken?
A poultry-geist.

Why did the chicken cross the road twice?
He was a double-crosser.

What's the difference between a chicken and an elephant?
An elephant can get chicken pox, but a chicken can't get elephant pox.

Why did the chicken cross the basketball court?
He heard the referee call fowl.

What do you call a frightened scuba diver?
Chicken of the sea.

What kind of tree does a chicken come from?
Poul-tree.

Why did the turkey cross the road?
The chicken had the day off.

What do you get when you cross a chicken with a guitar?
A chicken that makes music when you pluck it.

What do you call a joke book for chickens?
A yolk book.

7

How do you stop a rooster
from crowing on Friday?
Eat him on Saturday.

Which side of the chicken
has the most feathers?
The outside.

Why did the dinosaur
cross the road?
Chickens weren't
around.

Why did the chicken cross
the playground?
To get to the other slide.

What did the chicken do
when he saw the bucket of
fried chicken?
He kicked the bucket.

Why did the chicken cross the Internet?
To get to the other site.

Why did the cow cross the road?
To get to the udder side.

What do you call a witch that likes the beach, but is scared of the water?
A chicken sand-witch.

What do you call a chicken that crossed the road?
Poultry in motion.

# Laugh Out Loud

How do you catch a
runaway computer?
With an Internet.

Did you ever hear
the rope joke?
Skip it.

Did you ever see
a sidewalk?
No, but I've seen
a nose run.

Where do snowmen
keep their money?
In a snowbank.

Is it dangerous to swim
on a full stomach?
It's better to swim in
water.

What do you call a
deer with no eyes?
No idea.

Why is twice ten the
same as twice eleven?
Because twice ten is
twenty, and twice eleven
is twenty, too.

How do you fix a
cracked pumpkin?
With a pumpkin patch.

What should you do if
you swallow a spoon?
Lie down and don't stir.

What do computer
programmers eat for
a snack?
Chips.

How does Jack Frost
get around?
By icicle.

Why did the woman spray
her computer with insect
repellent?
A program had a bug in it.

What is made of wood,
but can't be sawed?
Sawdust.

What's bent, salty,
and sings?
Elvis Pretzel.

What animal lives
on your head?
A hare.

What has 12 hands,
6 eyes, 3 tails, and
can't see?
Three blind mice.

Where can you find
a lot of shoes?
In the foothills.

Why do you go to bed?
Because the bed won't
come to you.

What do porcupines
say when they kiss?
Ouch.

What do Eskimos
eat for breakfast?
Ice Krispies.

What do Alexander the
Great and Kermit the
Frog have in common?
The same middle name.

How do you find a lost dog?
Put your ear to a tree and
listen for the bark.

What's the hardest thing about riding a horse?
The ground.

What is hairy and writes?
A ballpoint bunny.

What kind of boats do smart kids travel on?
Scholar-ships

What driver has never passed a driving test?
A screwdriver.

When is it unlucky
to see a black cat?
When you're a mouse.

What animal drops
from the sky?
A rain deer.

What goes "99 bonk"?
A centipede with a
wooden leg.

What has 50 feet but
can't walk?
A tape measure.

What is black, white,
brown, and red all over?
A Chihuahua in a tuxedo
that fell into a jar of salsa.

16

Why did the fish
cross the ocean?
To get to the other tide.

Where do cows
go for fun?
The mooovies.

What is a cat's
favorite treat?
Mice Cream.

What kind of shoes
do frogs wear in
the summer?
Open toad sandals.

Why was the elephant
standing on the
marshmallow?
He didn't want to fall
in the hot chocolate.

What do you call
a fish with no eyes?
Fsh.

What do you call
a frog with no legs?
Unhoppy.

How do you know when
it's raining cats and dogs?
You step in a poodle.

What do you get
from a nervous cow?
A milk shake.

What did the 100 pound
parrot say?
"Polly want a cracker,
NOW!"

What do you call two
identically masked men?
The Clone Rangers.

What do you call a woman
with a frog on her head?
Lily.

If you have 5 noses,
6 ears, 4 mouths,
what are you?
UGLY!

What do you call two
bees, a hornet, and a wasp
with violins?
A sting quartet.

What do you get if you
cross a centipede with a
parrot?
A walkie-talkie.

# Knock, Knock

Knock, Knock
Who's there?
Anna.
Anna who?
Not Annather
knock, knock joke.

Knock, knock
Who's there?
Armageddon.
Armageddon who?
Armageddon outta here.

Knock, knock
Who's there?
Ben!
Ben who?
Ben knocking all day.

Knock, knock
Who's there?
Diss.
Diss who?
Diss is a dumb
knock, knock joke.

Knock, knock
Who's there?
A Fred.
A Fred who?
I was a fred you wouldn't
open the door.

Knock, knock
Who's there?
Dozen.
Dozen who?
Dozen anyone know
who I am?

Knock, knock
Who's there?
Lena.
Lena who?
Lena little closer
I have a secret.

Knock, knock
Who's there?
Noah.
Noah who?
Noah good place to eat?

Knock, knock
Who's there?
Ooze.
Ooze who?
Ooze in charge
around here!

Knock, knock
Who's there?
Midas.
Midas who?
Midas well let me in.

Knock, knock
Who's there?
Lettuce.
Lettuce who?
Lettuce in, it's cold
out here!

Knock, knock
Who's there?
Amiss.
Amiss who?
Amiss you! That's
why I'm here!

Knock, knock
Who's there?
Chicken!
Chicken who?
Chicken your pocket
for the keys.

Knock, knock
Who's there?
Wade.
Wade who?
Wade a minute,
I'll get the key!

Knock, knock
Who's there?
Ginger.
Ginger who?
Ginger hear the
doorbell?

Knock, knock
Who's there?
Belle.
Belle who?
Belle's not working
that's why I knocked.

Knock, knock
Who's there?
Fido.
Fido who?
Fido known you were
coming I would've
cleaned up.

Knock, knock
Who's there?
Havana.
Havana who?
Havana a great
time!

Knock, Knock
Who's there?
Juno.
Juno who?
I know who, do you
know who?

Knock, knock
Who's there?
Trish.
Trish who?
Bless you!


Knock, knock
Who's there?
Yul.
Yul who?
Yul see when you
open the door.


Knock, knock
Who's there?
Kent.
Kent who?
Kent you open the
door to find out?

Knock, knock
Who's there?
Frank.
Frank who?
Frank you for opening
the door!

Knock, knock
Who's there?
Guess Simon.
Guess Simon who?
Guess Simon knockin'
on the wrong door.

Knock, knock
Who's there?
Stella.
Stella who?
Stella same person who
was knocking before.

Knock, knock
Who's there?
Justin.
Justin who?
Justin time to let me in.

Knock, knock.
Who's there?
Ahmed.
Ahmed who?
Ahmed a mistake. Can I
borrow an eraser?

Knock, knock
Who's there?
Alex.
Alex who?
Alex the way you
wear your hair.

# Ghoulish Giggles

How do you talk to a monster?
Very carefully.

What's big and ugly and needs a big spoon of sugar?
A monster with the hiccups.

Why did the mummy go
to the drugstore?
He needed something
to help his coffin.

Why is monster
coffee so noisy?
Because they like
scream in it.

What is the shortest game
monsters know?
Swallow the leader.

What do you call a
vampire with no teeth?
Pointless.

What is the first thing you
should put into a haunted
house?
Someone else.

What do you call a monster
who writes a book?
An author.

What kind of dog does
Dracula have?
A bloodhound.

What has two heads, five
hands, a nose, and eight
feet?
A monster with
spare parts.

Where do ghouls
go to school?
Ghoullege.

Why did the monster
take his nose off?
To see what made it run.

How does a big, hairy monster climb a tree?
He sits on a seed and waits for it to grow.

What's green and weighs 200 lbs?
The Incredible Bulk.

What do you get if you cross a monster with a kangaroo?
Big holes in Australia.

Why are ghosts bad liars?
You can see right through them.

What kind of street does a ghost live on?
A dead end.

33

How do you know if a jokebook has monster jokes in it?
It gives you shivers up and down your spine.

What happens when a witch breaks the sound barrier?
You hear a sonic broom.

What do skeletons have nightmares of?
Dogs

How do you know if a werewolf has been in the fridge?
The huge paw prints in the butter.

What do you get when you cross a man-eating monster's path?
Eaten!

34

What is big, hairy, and has four wheels?
Bigfoot driving a car.

When do banshees howl?
On moanday night.

What makes more noise than an angry monster?
Two angry monsters.

Will a monster hurt you if
you run away from it?
It all depends on how
fast you run.

What do baby
monsters play with?
Deady Bears.

What do you get when
you cross Frankenstein
with a hot dog?
A Frankenfurterstein.

What is a banshee's
favorite game?
Hide and Shriek.

Does a monster need a menu
while on a cruise ship?
No, just the passenger list.

What do you get if you cross
King Kong with a frog?
A big gorilla that catches
planes with his tongue.

Why are skeletons
so calm?
Nothing gets under
their skin.

What would you find
on a haunted beach?
A sand witch.

What is a ghost's
favorite dessert?
Boo-berry pie and
I-scream.

What sound does a witch's
cereal make?
Snap, Cackle, Pop.

# School's In

What is sticky, purple, and is covered with thick hair? I don't know, but it sounds like lunch.

One good thing about this school cafeteria is you can eat dirt cheap.
But who wants to eat dirt?

Why does the cafeteria lady wear a white cap on her head?
Where else would she wear it?

Why are you eating your napkin?
Napkin?? That's why it tasted so much better than everything else.

What's worse than finding a worm in your school lunch?
Finding half a worm.

What is bacteria?
The back door to
the cafeteria.

Mmmmm...this bread is
nice and warm.
It should be. I've been
sitting on it all morning.

What's green and fuzzy
and sits on a bun?
The hamburger they serve in
the lunchroom.

What's the difference
between a pile of slugs
and school lunches?
School lunches are
on plates.

Teacher: You missed
school yesterday!
Student: Not really.

Why are you eating the school's cookies so fast?
I want to eat as many as I can before I lose my appetite.

Is that chili in your bowl?
Chilly? It's frozen solid.

What do catepillars taste like?
How should I know?
You just ate two of them in your lunch.

Murphy's Laws of the School Lunchroom
1. You will get a big piece of spinach stuck to your front tooth.
2. Someone will cut in front of you, and take the last decent looking pizza.
3. You'll drop your tray and everyone will cheer and applaud.
4. Your spoon will have brown stuff stuck to it.
5. The kid who talks with his mouth full will sit across from you.
6. Someone will make you laugh just as you start to drink your milk.

Did you hear about the student who couldn't write an essay about gold-fish?
He didn't have waterproof ink.

What would you get if you crossed a teacher with a vampire?
A lot of blood tests.

Teacher: "I hope I didn't see you copying off of John's test!"
Student: I hope you didn't either.

Where can you learn about ducks?
In the ducktionary!

How do you make seven an even number?
Take off the s.

How many letters are in the alphabet?
Eleven.
t-h-e-a-l-p-h-a-b-e-t

What is the easiest way to get a day off of school?
Wait until Saturday.

What word is always spelled wrong?
WRONG.

How many teachers does it take
to work the copier?
Who cares as long as they are
out of the classroom.

Where do martians
train to be teachers?
Mooniversity.

Why are teachers
like doctors?
Because both are good
at giving exams.

What did the teacher say
when he lost his pencil?
"Where's my pencil?"

Math teacher: What would you get
if you multiplied 1345 by 678?
Student: The wrong answer!

# School Excuse Extreme

My agent won't allow me to publish my homework until the movie deal is finalized.

Can you define "homework"?

Our furnace stopped working so we had to burn my homework so we wouldn't freeze.

Here it is. I wrote it in invisible ink.

I guess I dreamed I did it and turned it in.

I had an excuse, but I forgot it.

It was so perfect, I'm having it framed.

I got food poisoning from the school lunch, and I was physically unable to do my homework.

I was late for school because all the clocks in the house stopped at the same time.

I was doing my homework last night. I got up to get a drink from the kitchen. When I came back, my homework was gone, but I saw little green footprints leading under the bed.

I'm leading a protest to protect the trees.

Homework? I was supposed to bring it back to school? I thought it was supposed to stay at home.

My brother grabbed my homework by mistake.

I woke up this morning and couldn't remember anything. Who are you? Where am I? Who am I? What homework?

My parent's couldn't finish it, so they took it to work to get some help.

I'm translating it from Klingon.

I used it as scratch paper for my homework excuse list.

TEACHER EXCUSE:
I am sorry your tests are not all graded. The cat got jealous as I was marking instead of paying attention to him. After I went to bed, he attacked the test papers.

# The Doctor Is In!

Doctor, I feel as sick
as a dog!
Then, you should make an
appointment with a vet.

Doctor, I got trampled by
a bunch of cows.
I herd that!

Doctor, I think I have
a split personality.
Then, you'll have
to pay twice.

Doctor, I think I'm
an alligator.
Don't worry. You'll snap
out of it.

Doctor, I swallowed a
chicken bone!
Are you choking?
No, I'm serious.

Doctor, I have a button stuck up
my nose, what should I do?
Breathe through the
four little holes.

Doctor, I feel like $20.
Go shopping. The change will do you good.

Why does the dentist always seem sad?
Because he's always down in the mouth.

Student: I better send this math test to a doctor.
Teacher: Why?
Student: I just can't figure out the problems.

Doctor, can you get the quarter out of my ear?
Goodness, Why didn't you come to me sooner?
I didn't need the money until now.

Doctor, I have a fish in my ear!
I'm sending you to a specialist.
You have a serious herring problem.

Doctor, what should I do
if my ear rings?
Answer it!

Doctor, I have gas! What
should I do?
Go fill up my car.

What did the X-ray
of my head show?
Nothing.

Doctor, I think I'm
a calculator!
Then you should have
no problem taking your
math test.

Doctor, I swallowed my
harmonica!
Good thing you don't
play the piano.

Doctor, You have
to help me out!
Which way did you
come in?

Doctor, everyone
thinks I'm a liar.
That's hard to believe.

Doctor, I'm having
trouble breathing!
Don't worry. I'll put a
stop to that.

Doctor, I think
I need glasses!
You certainly do. This
is a restaurant.

Doctor, I feel like a yo-yo!
Oh? Feeling up and down?

Doctor, I broke my arm in two places.
Well don't go back to those places.

Doctor: I have some bad news and some worse news.
Patient: Give me the bad news.

Doctor: You have 24 hours to live.
Patient: What could be worse than that?
Doctor: I've been trying to reach you since yesterday.

A man walks into a doctor's office. He has a cucumber up his nose, a carrot in his left ear, and a banana in his right ear.
"What's the matter with me?" he asks the doctor.
The doctor says, "You're not eating right."

Doctor, I haven't stopped laughing since the operation! I told you I'd have you in stitches.

Why did the angry doctor have to retire? He lost his patients.

Doctor: I see you're reading the telephone book. Are you enjoying it? The plot is terrible, but what a cast of characters.

At the doctor's office, a woman touched her right knee with her index finger and yelled, "Ow, that hurts!" Then she touched her left cheek, and again yelled, "Ouch! That hurts, too." Then she touched her right earlobe, "Ow, even THAT hurts," she cried. The doctor looked at her a moment and said, "You have a broken finger."

# Sports Time

What lights up a
football stadium?
A football game.

What stories do
basketball players read?
Tall tales.

Where do ferris wheels
go in October?
The whirl series.

How are baseball games
and pancakes the same?
Both depend on
the batter.

When does a skier stop
going downhill?
When she reaches the
bottom.

What do you call a person
that tells bad jokes while
he's running?
A cross country punner.

Why was Cinderella such a
bad player?
Her coach was a pumpkin.

Why did the soccer ball
quit the team?
It was tired of being
kicked around.

What has 18 legs and
catches flies?
A baseball team.

What is the difference
between a baby and a
basketball player?
One drools and the
other dribbles.

Why did the volleyball go
to the bank?
It wanted to find its net
worth.

What should you do when 19
guys are running at you?
Throw the ball!

What are Brazilian soccer fans called?
Brazil nuts!

Why didn't the dog play baseball?
It was a boxer.

Why shouldn't you tell jokes while ice skating?
The ice might crack up.

Where do old bowling balls end up?
In the gutter.

What is the difference between a boxer and a man with a cold?
One knows his blows and the other blows his nose.

What has 22 legs and goes, "Crunch, crunch, crunch?"
A soccer team eating potato chips.

What race is never run?
A swimming race.

What is Wilt the Stilt's middle name?
The.

**Murphy's Sports Law:**
Exciting plays only happen when you're watching the scoreboard or buying a hot dog.

Why are wrestlers so
good at geometry?
They're used to circling
in a square ring.

What dessert should a
basketball player never eat?
Turnovers.

What position did the
monster play on the
soccer team?
Ghoulie.

Why do soccer players have trouble eating popcorn?
Because they can't use their hands.

What do you get if you cross a kung fu expert and a pig?
A pork chop.

Why did the ghost try out for the cheerleading squad?
To add a little team spirit.

What do you get if you cross a basketball player with a groundhog's shadow?
Six more weeks of baskeball season.

Two baseball teams played a game. One team won without a man touching home plate. How?
They were all-girl teams.

Who has played for every hockey team in the National Hockey League?
The organist at Madison Square Garden.

Why did the football player complain to the waiter?
There was a fly in his soup-er bowl.

Sports Reporter: How long have you been running?
Track Star: Since I was eight years old.
Sports Reporter: Wow! You must be tired.

What do you get if you
cross a karate expert with
a tree?
Spruce Lee.

What do you get if you
lock two bikes together?
Siamese Schwinns.

What do you call a boomerang
that doesn't come back?
A stick.

What do pigs do when
they play basketball?
They hog the ball.

Where is the headquarters of
the Umpires' Association?
The Umpire State Building.

What do you call the football player who guesses the other team's plays?
The hunchback.

Why does a baseball pitcher raise one leg?
If he raised both legs, he'd fall down.

Where should a baseball team never wear red?
In the bullpen.

What's black and white, and sticky all over?
A referee who fell in the Sugar Bowl.

What's black and white, and green all over?
A referee who fell in the Gator Bowl.

# Reading is Fun!

How To Reach the Top
by Stan Dupp

Talking to Children
by Neil Down

Basketball Bloopers
by Dub L. Dribble

The Sting
by B. Keeper

Jail Break
by Freida Prizner

Famous Knockouts
by Seymour Stars

Close Shaves
by Ray Zerr

The Millionaire
by Iva Fortune

World Atlas
by Joe Graffie

Hockey Plays
by I.C. Tose

A Ghost in the Attic
by Howie Wales

Speaking Spanish
by Lorna Lang
Wedge

A Terrible Nightmare
by Gladys Over

Famous People
by Hugh Did-Watt

The Haunted House
by Hugo Furst

Infectious Disease
by Willie Catchet

A Hole in the Roof
by Lee King

Long Winter's Night
by I.M. Freezin

Sahara Journey
by Rhoda Camel

The Hurricane Blows
by Gail Forse

Dealing with Bullies
by Howard U. Lykett

Swimming the
English Channel
by Francis Neer

Horror Classics
by R.U. Scared

The Arctic Ocean
by Cole Waters

Growing Rice
by Patty Fields

The Mad Cat
by Claude Boddy

The Long Walk
to School
by Misty Bus

# Crazy Animals

Why do elephants never get rich?
Because they work for peanuts.

What has 500 pairs of sneakers, a ball, and two hoops?
A centipede basketball team.

What do you get if you
cross Bambi with a ghost?
Bamboo.

What do you call a crate
of ducks?
A box of quackers.

What do termites have
for dessert?
Toothpicks.

What is the best way to
catch a monkey?
Climb a tree and act like
a banana.

What's the difference
between a mouse and
an elephant?
About a ton.

73

What kind of music is
played in the jungle?
Snake, rattle, and roll.

What do vultures always
have for dinner?
Leftovers.

What do you call
a bull taking a nap?
A bull dozer.

What do you get if
you cross a small dog
with a frog?
A croaker spaniel.

What do you call a mouse
that can pick up an elephant?
Sir!

What is the biggest ant in the world?
Eleph-ant.

What is even bigger?
A gi-ant!

How many ants are needed to fill an apartment?
Ten-ants.

Where do ants eat?
A restaur-ant.

Why don't anteaters get sick?
Because they are full of ant-ibodies.

What do you get if you cross a leopard with a watchdog?
A terrified postal carrier.

What's small, squeaks, and hangs out in caves?
Stalagmice.

When is a car like a frog?
When it's being toad.

What's the difference between a mosquito and a fly?
Try zipping a mosquito.

What is the difference between a lion and a tiger?
A tiger has the mane part missing.

What did the frog say when he had a cold?
I feel like I have a person in my throat.

What is a scared farmyard creature?
A chicken.

What is the tallest yellow flower in the world?
A Giraffodil!

What do you call a large gray animal that's just eaten a ton of beans?
A smellyphant!

What is big and gray, and good at math?
An elephant with a calculator.

What do you do with a green elephant?
Wait until he's ripe.

Where do rabbits learn to fly planes?
In the hare force.

What is the best way to contact a fish?
Drop him a line.

What happened to the frog's car when it broke down?
It was toad away.

What's black and white, black and white, and black and white?
A penguin rolling down a hill.

Why did the elephant paint the bottom of his feet yellow?
So he could hide in the vanilla pudding.

Did you ever see an elephant in vanilla pudding?
No? Then it must work.

What kind of sharks never eat women?
Man-eating sharks.

What did the snail say when he hitched a ride on the turtle's back?
Weeeeeeeeee!!!!!!

What's big, white, furry, and found in the outback of Australia?
A very lost Polar Bear.

# Jokes-a-plenty

What do you get if you cross a zombie with a Boy Scout?
A creature that scares old ladies across the street.

Why did the girl put a chicken
in a pot of boiling water?
She wanted the chicken to lay
hard-boiled eggs.

Why did the cat sit
on the computer?
To keep an eye on
the mouse.

What is yellow and
highly dangerous?
Shark infested
pudding.

Why should you never
tell secrets in a cornfield?
Because you are
surrounded by ears!

What do you get if you
cross a bird with a snake?
A feather boa constrictor!

How do you know if
your school bus is old?
The seats are covered
in mammoth hide.

Did you hear about the boy
that put his grandmother's
dentures under his pillow?
The tooth fairy left him a
fake $10 bill.

How do you
cut water?
With a sea-saw!

What is the difference
between electricity
and lightning?
Lightning is free.

Why did the author
write on her foot?
She was writing
a footnote.

Why was the genie of
the lamp angry?
Someone rubbed him
the wrong way!

What is the best thing
to do when a hippo
sneezes?
Get out of the way!

When are you allowed
to take gum to school?
On chews-day!

Why did the silly school
buy a sea horse?
Because they wanted
to play water polo.

Why did the farmer
feed his pigs sugar
and vinegar?
He wanted sweet
and sour pork.

Thirty people were
huddled under an
umbrella. How many
got wet?
None—it wasn't
raining.

What do you call a
dinosaur that keeps
you awake at night?
A Bronto-snore-us

Why do you
always paint
rivers and lakes?
Because I'm using
watercolors.

What do you call a
happy mushroom?
Fun Gus!

What happens if
you jump into the
Red Sea with a
white bathing suit?
You get wet.

Who held a baby
octopus for ransom?
Squidnappers.

How do you spell
mousetrap using
only three letters?
C-A-T.

What did the postage
stamp say to the
envelope?
Stick with me and
we'll go places.

What do you get if
you cross a monster
with a cat?
No stray dogs for a
2 mile radius.

What is the capital
of Australia?
A.

What kind of trees
are deck chairs made
from?
Beach trees!

What has four
legs and flies?
A two pair of
pants.

Where is the only
place on Earth where
Friday comes before
Thursday?
A dictionary!

Why did the lion
spit out the clown?
Because he tasted
funny.

How many programmers
does it take to screw in a
lightbulb?
None, it's a hardware
problem.

What kind of ship
never sinks?
Friendship.

What flies around
all day, but never
goes anywhere?
A flag.

What kind of coat do you put on only when it is wet?
A coat of paint.

What is purple, 5,000 years old, and 1,500 miles long?
The Grape Wall of China

Why was the broom late?
It overswept.

Where did the king keep his armies?
Up his sleevies.

# Food for Thought

Waiter, there's a fly in
my soup!
Shhh! Or everyone
will want one.

Waiter, there is a bee
in my soup!
Of course, it's alphabet
soup.

What cereal do
rappers eat?
Cheeri-Yo-Yo-Yo!

Waiter, what's the insect
in my soup?
I don't know. I'm a wait-
er, not an entomologist.

Waiter, there's a fly in
my soup!
No sir, that's just dirt
in the shape of a fly.

Waiter, I don't see
chocolate cake on
the menu!
No sir, I wiped
it off!

Waiter, there are two
flies in my soup!
That's ok, the extra
one is free.

Waiter, your thumb
is in my soup!
That's ok, it's
not hot.

Waiter, there's a
mosquito in my
soup!
I'm sorry. We've
run out of flies.

Waiter, there is a fly
in my soup!
Don't worry, the
frog should
surface any
minute.

Waiter, I can't eat this!
Why not sir?
Because you haven't given me a knife and fork.

Waiter, there is a small slug in my salad!
I'm sorry ma'am, would you like a bigger one?

Waiter, there is a spider on my food!
I'm sorry, no pets allowed.

Waiter, what is this cockroach doing in my ice cream?
Skiing!

Waiter, there's a frog in
my soup!
He must be looking for
the fly.

Waiter, why is your
hand on my steak?
You don't want it
to fall on the floor
again, do you?

Waiter, will the
pancakes be long?
No, round.

What was the reporter
doing at the ice cream
shop?
Getting the scoop.

Did you hear about the restaurant on the moon?
Great food, but no atmosphere.

How many fast food workers does it take to change a lightbulb?
Two. One to change it and one to add fries.

How many lunchroom ladies does it take to change a lightbulb?
None. It's better not to see the food.

Waiter, bring me something
to eat and make it snappy!
How about an
alligator sandwich?

Waiter! There are 49
flies in my soup!
One more and we'll
have a world record!